TEACHINGS FOR YOU AND YOUR KIDS

RISE BEFORE IT'S TOO LATE

Let's Focus On The Things That Matter

Nikhil P. Bhandare

INDIA • SINGAPORE • MALAYSIA

ISBN

Paperback 979-8-89415-382-7

Hardcase 979-8-89475-021-7

CONTENTS

SPECIAL THANKS

Writing a book is a challenging endeavour, but equally demanding is the task of proofreading, suggesting improvements, and rectifying errors. In this journey, I am deeply grateful to several individuals whose support and contributions have been invaluable.

First and foremost, I extend my heartfelt gratitude to my father, Mr. Pramod B. Bhandare, a retired Government ITI Principal, whose unwavering dedication to delving into the depth of concepts has pushed me to bring more clarity to the content. I am also indebted to my wife, Dr. Dipali N. Bhandare, for her support and understanding throughout this journey.

Additionally, I am immensely thankful to my friends who have generously shared their insights and expertise. Special mention goes to Mr. Ravi Meshram, Officer at NABARD, Mr. Muppalla Prudhvi Raj, Technical Manager at R&D, Systems, Central Electronics Limited, and Mrs. A D Bhargavi, Senior Team Lead at Content and Publications, Study IQ, for their valuable contributions.

The collaborative effort of my family and friends has undoubtedly enriched the content of this book. I extend my sincere appreciation to each one of them for their invaluable input and commitment.

INSPIRATION

This book is an attempt to explain the present situation of the world and how to thrive in such circumstances. I find that the people we live with, the socio-economic system we operate in, and the many influences we encounter through media—movies, songs, advertisements, social media, etc.—are taking us away from the things that really matter. I have observed and analysed life and have come to my own understanding of life in the current era. I undertook this project of writing a book so that I could collate all my observations and pass them on to my recently born daughter. I hope that the wisdom I have collected and shared through this book will help her live a better life. And as that happens, this book will also help other people, especially young parents like me, who might be wondering what to teach kids about life. So, if you also feel that we are spending much of our attention on things that don't matter, then let's explore what is wrong and how we can protect ourselves from all the things that don't matter.

PREFACE

It is necessary to keep some ideas alive. It is necessary to hand over valuable knowledge to the curious souls and the next generations, especially in this fast-moving, fast-changing world where people have less time for self-development and self-analysis. Work and other distractions have robbed people of their time. However, somewhere, people themselves are also responsible for not finding time for their own sake. Lack of discipline, wrong ideas of living, and wrong mindsets are taking them away from the 'things that matter'. Many feel that life has become meaningless. To some extent, this is true if one does not make the necessary efforts to improve it.

I decided to write this book to pass on my analysis of life and crucial ideas regarding living to the readers, including my recently born daughter. The world is what it is. It is being shaped by a majority, under various influences. Life choices, socially decided ideas of progress, values, preferences, and aspirations of the majority determine the parameters of 'what is right and what is wrong'. What is popular may not be right, and what is right may not always be popular. This is what is happening nowadays. When lies are repeated over and over, they appear true. And unfortunately, many non-enlightened souls believe in such lies and waste their lives by living these lies, drifting away from the things that matter.

On the other hand, there are some individuals facing challenges in their quest for self-development and understanding the essence of life. This book serves as evidence that there is a community dedicated to personal growth. Readers will glean insights from its contents, recognising they are not solitary in their journey and will resonate with its concepts.

It is not that the knowledge presented in this book or any other good book is unique. Throughout history, many good writers have presented useful knowledge in their own expressions and languages. Readers will find some reference to particular knowledge in one book or another. However, what remains interesting or worth reading is the analysis of that knowledge and the way it is expressed. The same is the case with this book as well.

Also, some of the ideas may appear controversial, against the popular trend, and at times extremist. I understand that they may not be received very well. I was hesitant to share those in this book. But when I see my daughter, I ponder if she should know about those ideas. Then, the answer is yes because those ideas are nearer to the truth. Hence, I have included such ideas in this book. It may also happen that you would disagree with such ideas. In such cases, let's just agree to disagree.

This book provides my study about life, mind, God, progress, development, and the present state of the world to those who may need it. We have to protect ourselves and our children from incorrect education. This book is my humble attempt to safeguard my daughter and others from the pitfalls of misinformation. In its pages, may she find guidance amidst life's uncertainties, and may this knowledge endure as my legacy, nurturing minds for generations to come.

INTRODUCTION

This book falls into the 'Self Help' category, or we may also call it the 'Self-Development' category. There are many books and videos available in this category. People have slowly started to understand that 'Self-development' is necessary to bring positive changes in life. Sometimes, we find ourselves in difficult situations—such as unemployment, low scores in exams, bad habits, health issues, failures, etc.—and we want to get out of those situations. In such circumstances, we need certain clarity and focus to improve our lives. And in such circumstances, 'Self-help' content helps a lot.

I don't mean to say that we should engage with 'Self-Help Content' only if we are in difficult situations. These are generally useful for leading an enthusiastic, energetic, and easy life.

At this moment, I would also like to draw your attention to why we should read.

Our being and quality of life depend on our knowledge and awareness. This knowledge and awareness are like a shrinking space. The knowledge and awareness we develop naturally deteriorate over time. If we don't revise or actively try to expand this space, it will shrink faster than we think. And if that shrinks, then it will affect our overall well-being and life. One can experience this with the general observation that when one revisits an old, already-read book, she will realise that she had learnt so much from that book earlier but forgot some of the learnings. Hence, regular reading is necessary to keep our knowledge and awareness relevant. Understand that good knowledge fades away, hence one needs to keep reading good books regularly.

I have studied life in my capacity, read various books, and watched various videos to improve my mind, thinking patterns, and overall mindset. Among all the resources, I found YouTube videos by 'Ben Lionel Scott' very relevant and close to the truth. Ideas shared by him are also inculcated in this book.

We can generate our own ideas only from our existing knowledge and awareness. As ideas are generated from our own space of awareness, they may fail to provide an 'out of the box' perspective since we generate ideas from our perspective itself. Of course, with some focus and deliberation, we can generate new ideas, but getting new ideas becomes easier if we read. You may not easily think outside of your own mind, and you will need the help of ideas not generated by yourself to get a fresh perspective.

Read to get inspired by ideas. Reading is one of the methods, an easier and more comfortable one, to get new ideas and to develop ourselves. Being a private affair, we are alone while reading, which gives the reader comfort to interpret and analyse the text, learn from it, and build perspectives. This process also builds the mindset.

Most of you may be aware that the world has become a place of distractions. Reading can also help in diverting our minds to something better. Additionally, in this process, we can also gain some wisdom.

This is a book of ideas; ideas that are relevant and timeless. I hope you will get some fresh perspectives while reading this book. Even after a significant gap, like 1-5 years, between the last and next reads, you will find it relevant.

Don't be afraid of forgetting. Just remember to read and come back to the wisdom. You will forget many of the ideas in the rush of life. But you will feel the urge to relearn ideas and wisdom, and you will revisit the ideas derived from truth again and again, in one form or another, through this book or another medium.

Section 1: Current Situation of The World

Chapter 1

NEGATIVITY IN THE PRESENT WORLD – THE RISE OF STUPIDITY

First, I would like to explain the present state of the world. I don't intend to generalise, as the whole world is not entirely negative or dark, but one needs to be aware of what I am going to present.

What is the present state of the world and how to go through it?

The present world is tough. One doesn't get success easily. There is high inequality, resources are not distributed evenly, and life is really unfair to many. Some people are disoriented, and many ideas of living, enjoyment, joy, and progress are corrupted. Finding true wisdom and living by those right ideas has become tough due to distractions, temptations, peer pressure, and an overall negative pull force. This is the world of 'Maya' (Illusion). You alone must pull yourself together.

Self-discipline, self-protection (mental and physical), self-motivation, good habits, remembering the wisdom, and staying on the right track are the only options. You will have to do it for yourself. You must choose to live on the right track, develop the will for genuine and true progress, and you will have to develop a love for wisdom. Everyone's life is different; each one faces different situations, and this is your life. No one will know what is in store for you. No one will know what you are going through. You just have to find your way through it.

There are educated and self-aware people in the world, and there are those who are unaware and lost. At the core, it is the development of the mind and self that differentiates these categories. Studying psychology and philosophy helps a person develop a better mindset, which in turn gives them the power to progress in this world. When we talk about mindsets in the present world, yes, due to a lack of awareness of psychology and philosophies, a lot of negativity exists. Unaware people are trapped in ignorance. They are not educated enough to understand the importance of a 'positive mindset'. Moreover, if anyone desires to practice positive thinking to improve themselves, they are often mocked and thus discouraged.

Negativity has risen in many forms nowadays, such as stupidity, drama, discouragement, unwarranted complaints, and becoming a crybaby. You will starkly experience negativity when you enter the job market.

I will explain some elements of negativity in the world –

- Complaining and crying about life situations, such as bad luck, a bad day, or a bad phase.
- Complaining rather than being grateful for their job. You will find such people in every organisation, and they are often in the majority.
- Being less enthusiastic.
- No drive for adventure. People have become risk-averse, though it is okay to take calculated risks.
- Not trying hard enough to improve their situation and somehow hoping that time and situation will change without taking necessary actions.
- Engaging in self-pity and behaving like a victim.
- Highlighting the negatives of what they have rather than looking at the positives.
- Rampantly discouraging others through various means such as mocking, making fun, ignoring, and jealousy.

- The rise of stupidity and cult mentality.
- Finding enjoyment and entertainment in self-destructive habits and behaviours, such as excessive alcohol consumption, late-night lifestyles, drugs, and smoking. This is a totally wrong interpretation of joy and enjoyment. Stay away from temptations and addictive habits. They will consume your time and mind without you even realising it. This path leads to downfall and guilt later on. The mind should be free and progressive. Only then can one feel fulfillment.
- A huge rise in distractions is preventing individuals from enjoying their own company or the company of their own mind. The principle of 'Live and let live' has become a matter of the past.
- A rise in the toxicity of relationships—both personal and professional. Petty grudges, ego issues, or minor differences can create rifts in relationships.
- Revenge-taking tendencies, in varying intensities, are consuming some of the energy and focus of minds.

The list is not exhaustive. You may identify or have experienced some of the negative tendencies mentioned above, either in yourself or within your circle. Possessing these elements is not the right way of living.

With your hard work, consistency, and luck, you will achieve some success. You will have resources and lead a good life. However, the world doesn't always take your success, abundance, and happiness positively. It will try to find faults in your life or attempt to discourage you, or make you feel inadequate by suggesting that you should have more of this or that. It will not let you live in peace unless you shut some doors and protect yourself. Thanks to social media, you will also face temptations to disclose or show off your success and wealth to others. But don't. Keep your achievements a huge secret. There is no need to disclose what you have. Make secrecy a habit. As simple as that.

One phrase was very popular in Indian cinema merely two decades ago. The idea was, "Khushiyaan baatne se badhti hai aur dukh baatne se kam hota hai", meaning, "Happiness increases when shared, and sadness decreases when shared". But in the present world, there is a significant departure from this earlier position, and the opposite is happening. When you share happiness, it decreases (there will be jealousy, disbelief, or there will be evil eyes), and when you share sadness, it increases (as some will make fun of your weaknesses instead of helping you or try to frighten you with your present situation and make you do things that will benefit them). So, my simple advice is to strengthen yourself, help yourself, and try to keep things as secret as possible.

Beware of Maya, the illusion!

What should be disgusted is promoted, and what should be promoted is disgusted. This is the Maya! Let us ponder over the concept of 'Maya'. Maya means 'Illusion'. This is an old concept, yet a difficult one to understand and probably not very well understood. The general understanding of the concept is:

'Things are not what they look like.'

Now, there can be varied interpretations of this phrase. Does it mean that what we perceive through our senses is not true? Does it mean that everything we see and hear is a lie? Does it mean that everything we see, feel, taste, and hear has a deeper meaning?

Another popular phrase is 'Sab Moh Maya hai', meaning 'Everything is an illusion'. This phrase somewhere indicates that there is no meaning in anything. This suggests that money is useless, keeping your discipline is useless, your achievements are useless, it is okay to "have fun" (whatever interpretation of this term) and let go, etc. These types of interpretations are very dangerous. Such ideas misguide us to lose hope, to be lazy, to give up, and not to try anything new.

When I started thinking about the concept of Maya, the above 'well-known and well-accepted definitions' appeared shallow. As per my analysis, the concept of Maya need not actually be understood at a physical or material level but should be applied at a mental or thinking level. And it has a lot to do with the choices we make.

In my understanding, when we say that this world is an illusion, it means that by default we are lost—directionless, we do not know where we are, or where we are going. We do not know where we should go, or what we should do. It means that we are not doing self-analysis, we are not analysing life, we are not analysing what we are doing with life and our overall existence.

Many don't know how to live and how to think.

Living under the wrong influence is Maya! Whatever you are being told, taught, guided with, and given input of, you need to scrutinize.

The Maya or illusion is in the form of –

1. Wrong thinking and mindset.
2. Wrong ideas and knowledge.
3. Wrong culture.
4. Wrong influences.

5. Too many distractions by various agencies.
6. Wrong options and availing wrong choices.
7. Wrong interpretations.
8. Remaining unfocused.

We will analyse further the concept of 'Maya'. On a deeper level, we can say that the world is an illusion because there is an increasing tendency among people to chase things that don't matter, to get bothered about things that don't matter, to take focus away from mind development, and to get influenced by propaganda, among other things. The list can go on.

In other words, the changed priorities of the people in favour of the following can also be understood as Maya or illusion –

- Show-offs.
- Remaining greedy.
- To be socially acceptable.
- To be admired.

Whether life is on the right track or the wrong track, you need to analyse yourself. And if you think that you are on the wrong track, then you are living in Maya.

These, in my opinion, are deeper and truer interpretations of the word Maya or illusion. In this context, the world is an illusion. This illusion has created certain negativity in the world. We will discuss this as we go along.

It is not that good things are absent. Due to this 'Maya' (illusion), the world has become such that good things are ignored and not given importance. The good things are hidden in plain sight. They are everywhere, but we are not able to see them. Enlightening knowledge is readily available but not sought after. Too many distractions and many unnecessary things consume your time and energy.

People adopt negativity because it is influential and abundant. In all probability, one will encounter negativity before positivity. In all likelihood, one will face discouragement before receiving encouragement. Typically, one will encounter criticism for something at the first instance rather than praises when asked for an opinion about anything. More often than not, one will hear how something is bad first rather than the opportunities that exist in it. And if negativity is so abundant, people adapt to negativity to blend in, to remain socially acceptable. But remember, what is popular is not always right, and what is right is not always popular.

Creation of Needs

Commercials, branding, and marketing agencies have created artificial needs through innovative and creative content. They are constantly engaged in propaganda, telling lies to influence your thinking and making you believe that you really need their products. Understand your true and real needs. Shut the doors to undue influences and fears from these agencies.

The rise of stupidity and cult mentality

The ideas and debates related to religion, politics, leaders, celebrity lifestyles, and comparisons that people engage in nowadays reflect a general rise in stupidity worldwide. They are simply drifting away from 'the things that matter' to 'irrelevant topics'. Shield yourself from stupidity. Most of the discussions and debates that generally occur in our society are irrelevant; ignore them. As discussed in the last chapter of this book, build your own island and cut off from the stupidity of the world.

Also, some followers of leaders or institutions are so brainwashed that they don't realise they have developed a cult mentality. They become totally blind and always try to make others believe in their ideology. This is where they waste their energy. That cult becomes their identity. Sometimes, you might get shaken by their confidence and devotion. But come back to yourself and come back to the truth. Do and think what is really true for you.

Let others be protectors or champions of culture, religion, and heritage, and let them feel proud and all macho about it. You do what is logical and suits you. Never let these cult people influence your decision.

Now, many would disagree with me here, but let us just agree to disagree.

Don't have much hopes from the education system either.

Don't have high hopes for the 'education system'. Very few educational institutes are clear about the kind of minds they aim to develop and adhere to those standards. Meanwhile, other education institutes are themselves confused about the kind of minds to be developed. The bad thing is that they might educate—or more accurately, brainwash—you with the wrong things, such as imposing personal preferences concerning politics, leaders, or religion by teachers or institutes! They are, in a way, drifting away from the truth and what truly matters. The presence of faulty education and bad influence is more prevalent than good education and good influence. You have to learn your stuff yourself. Take help when necessary but keep your filters on. Don't get influenced by others if they are not true. Verify your inputs.

Another issue is that teachers who have faulty ideas of modernity may merely project these onto kids, hampering their true mind development and disorienting them, thus pushing them into Maya!

I came across a good question in a movie that helps clear undue influence. The question is 'According to whom?'. That's it. Ask this question whenever you see a commercial or come across any suggestion or idea. It will help you find the right intentions.

Albert Einstein is quoted as saying: "Stay away from negative people. They have a problem for every solution." Whereas, positive people tend to find solutions to every problem. To keep moving forward, we need to find solutions to existing problems and progress. However, if you are stuck with a negative person or team, you will not be able to move ahead. You will meet many people who fit the description given by Mr. Einstein. Probably, the truth is that they don't want to move ahead or don't want to see others move ahead.

Be in that company or relationship which brings the best out of you, not the worst out of you.

Otherwise, stay alone and focus on improvement and making life better.

We are witnessing changing definitions of joy and enjoyment due to the influence of movies, songs, advertisements, and social media. The environment is being created where joy and enjoyment mean less work, a lot of parties, social validations, showing off wealth, remaining undisciplined, and spending too much money, among other things.

But do you know where real joy and enjoyment are found? They are in discipline, self-development, work, focus, health, singing, art, and struggle—the very things which people often try to avoid.

Again, I will mention, what should be disgusted is promoted, and what should be promoted is disgusted. Understand what Maya has done to our mindsets.

Yes, technology has made our lives easier and helped us achieve great feats. However, for those who are not self-aware and self-disciplined, technology is also causing the problem of distractions. Every now and then, screens are bombarded with random videos, random advertisements, bad influences, or objectionable content. From 2022 to 2024, there has been an unnecessary dominance of 'online card games' and 'tobacco' advertisements on TV and YouTube. Surprisingly, many big celebrities are endorsing and promoting these activities, which can lead to bad habits.

See, you can't really rely on anyone for guidance nowadays!

Socialising norms are also changing in the present world, especially in the workplace where socialisation has turned toxic for juniors. The rising trend at the workplace is to make fun of and demoralise others, especially juniors, in a process often referred to as "roasting". Under the pretext of fun, they will offend you, potentially breaking your heart. The expectation is that you should not be angry or feel offended. This culture is really weird! If you need to protect your self-respect, then keep your interactions to a minimum and avoid disclosing your ideas when you encounter such negative people, groups, or within WhatsApp/ social media communities.

This was my attempt to demonstrate some of the dominant negative tendencies in the world. I don't mean to say that the whole world is a bad place, but one needs to be aware of these issues. It may also be possible that, in a subtle way, you all have experienced these negative tendencies in various life situations and hence you are able to relate to them. It's just that you may not have noted these down or simply have chosen to ignore them. However, I kept track of it and could list some major elements. But that is enough negativity for the book. From the next chapter onwards, we will discuss mind development, things that matter in life, how to improve life, and more.

Section 2: Relation Between Mind And Our Surrounding

Chapter 2
MIND PURIFICATION

Having read so much about negativity, let us explore what mind purification is. Back in 2011, when I was undergoing a Vipassana meditation course, I asked my teacher what the purpose of meditation was. He answered that the purpose of meditation is to 'purify the mind'. At the time, I didn't quite understand what he meant. But now, I understand this concept and will share it with you.

Mind purification means to make the mind free of "dirt and poisons". When we do not pay attention to our mind, we fail to remain aware of the "dirt and poisons" that accumulate on it. The dirt on the mind refers to self-limiting thoughts, fear, a sense of victimhood or injustice, lack of enthusiasm, diminished interest, ungratefulness, and unnecessary complaining. Meanwhile, poison in the mind refers to harbouring an evil eye for someone, ill intentions, engaging in conspiracies, or harbouring hatred for something.

When we 'unknowingly' carry this dirt and poison in our minds, we do not live life to its full potential; we remain trapped with that dirt and poison. We cannot think clearly, and having dirt or poison in our mind is somehow anti-life.

We will study more about the mind and its role in our quality of life in the next chapter. But understand that the mind is like the software and CPU of our existence. Purifying, if not controlling, the mind is the starting point for improving life.

I will provide two good instances which signify the importance of mind purification:

a. 'Peaceful Warrior': In this movie, the centuries-old teacher Socrates teaches Dan about the importance of clearing the mind. He describes "the trash" as anything that keeps us from focusing on what truly matters—the present moment. Negative beliefs from our past and our fears and uncertainties about the future can prevent us from making the most of the present, and we need to let them go. Socrates emphasises, "And when you truly are in the here and now, you'll be amazed at what you can do, and how well you can do it."

b. What Saint (Sant) Tukaram said: Saint Tukaram, a revered figure, once stated, "Mann Kara Re Prasanna, Sarva Siddhiche Kaaran." This translates to, "Make your mind fresh (purified), as it is the cause of all prosperity and achievements." Through this, he conveys that the prosperity and achievements we observe are often the results of having an enthusiastic, fresh, and happy mind.

Meditation and self-analysis

When discussing mind purification, it's inevitable that we touch on the topic of meditation. Meditation has become a buzzword. There are many ideas and perceptions associated with meditation, but not all of them are accurate. Some claims, such as 'meditation improves memory' or 'meditation quickly improves life', are often exaggerated to influence people to start practising meditation. Whether the ends justify these means is debatable. Let's explore some other common misconceptions about meditation:

1. It is for the later part of life.
2. Meditative people don't get angry.
3. If someone is getting angry, then they are not doing the right meditation.
4. A particular meditation practice is better than the others.
5. People who practice meditation cannot do any wrong.
6. High moral and otherwise expectations from people who practice meditation, testing

their patience at every step. And when they react to provocations, critics will just prove the point that meditation is not yielding the desired results.

7. Not able to find time for practising meditation.
8. People can develop superhuman capabilities at advanced stages of meditation.
9. Meditation has been branded as magic that can automatically enhance your mood, calm your mind, and bring wealth, etc.
10. Meditation involves the complete eradication of thoughts.

In my opinion, we need to ignore all these perceptions and try to understand meditation on our own. Also, I am of the opinion that meditation and self-analysis go hand in hand. Meditation is my time, my zone, away from the whole world—a zone to remember what needs to be remembered, to settle down thoughts, conduct self-analysis, analyse current situations, pray, and converse with God, etc. Indeed, it is true that meditation brings heart-filled satisfaction (which naturally resets our mood) and clarity, which helps in better resolves. These results may indirectly help in bringing other material benefits.

I wish that 'meditation' should be hyphenated with 'self-analysis'.

❖❖❖

We need mind purification more often than we think. Mind purification is like a reset button—a reset of mood, thoughts, perceptions, and, most importantly, the level of enthusiasm. Complaining, crying, whining, and ungratefulness are indications of a temporarily polluted mind. We all experience this at times, and it is okay. However, it is crucial to recognise when the mind has been polluted and needs to be purified, needs a reset. This is important to actually move forward from whatever situation you are in.

A temporarily, and more so permanently, dirty or impurified mind is like a wheel stuck in the mud—unable to move and causing trouble to us. The emotions that rush through us when our minds are polluted are indications that we need to change something in our lives. It may be our attitude (the way we see things), our daily schedule, our company, or our connection level with our inner self.

A purified mind, on the other hand, is full of enthusiasm, forward-looking, solution-oriented, and excited for the situations that arise.

The will to transition from an impurified mind to a purified mind is the real deal. Many people lack this will. Essentially, they do not want to purify their minds and remain in that particular mental/emotional state for a long time. This may be due to lethargy or external pressures and influences. However, one thing is clear: there is no point in remaining in a low mental/emotional state.

In my opinion, learning the transition of the mind from impure to pure is one of the things that matter in life. And this lesson is straightforward. First, we need to realise that we are in a low or negative mental/emotional state. After understanding the triggers, we need to be willing to shift our mental state. The will to shift the mental state will arise if we can appreciate the knowledge that it is necessary to be in a good mental/emotional state. Remember this knowledge in times of need. And then, the transition begins at that particular moment. It is the beginning of a transformation. Think about how you can come out of the situation (solution orientation), make a rough plan to emerge from that, use a diary to track progress/ journey, motivate yourself, etc.

Based on this knowledge of mind purification and self-analysis, one can broadly identify two emotional states: one is a relaxed and happy mood state, and the other is a tense, grudge-ridden, pain-bearing mood state. We need to understand that when there is dirt in the mind (in the form of thoughts, general laziness, or some sort of complaint), then there will be a negative emotional state. Once we identify it, we need to remove the dirt from the mind. Sometimes, removing dirt from the mind is not an immediate process, but with practice, one can learn to remove it fairly quickly.

In the book 'The Laws of the Spirit World' by Khorshed Bhavnagri, it is mentioned that God helps those who help themselves. This is profound knowledge and a universal truth. So be ready to help yourself first in all situations. The subsequent journey becomes magical and pleasant if you decide to help yourself. This knowledge, nevertheless, has been expressed by many other guides/gurus too, like Chanakya. This book is merely another medium to bring that knowledge to you, and if you have come across this knowledge again, then it is an indication that you should remember it.

A purified mind will accept the situation as it is, and if there are dangers or challenges, it will try to find solutions. Naturally, due to the difficulties faced, some negative thoughts will enter the mind; let us call these thoughts 'dirt'. When we are aware of the concept of 'mind purification', we will immediately start the mind-cleaning process and replace the 'dirt-causing thoughts' with positive thoughts. Depending on the difficulties faced and the trauma they have caused, the dirt removal and the process of replacing it with positive thoughts may take some time. But eventually, when we have a positive mindset, things start improving.

It has been difficult to define what positive thinking and a positive mindset are. We can only list certain elements of them. A positive mindset and positive thinking help us in purifying the mind. The non-exhaustive list of elements that demonstrate positive thinking and a positive mindset includes:

- Useful thinking is positive thinking, contrary to useless thinking which doesn't lead us anywhere.
- There is a genuine intention to improve one's life.
- There is a hunger for wisdom.
- There is zeal to conquer challenges.
- Willingness to take action to achieve goals.
- There is a sense of adventure.
- Ambitious outlook.

Albert Einstein once said, "The most important decision we make is whether we believe we live in a friendly or a hostile universe."

When our mind is purified, we believe that the universe is friendly, and when there is (temporary) impurity in the mind, we believe that we live in a hostile universe.

Impurity of the mind, in the form of dirt or poison, will harm you by preventing you from seeing things that matter. You will live under the influence of false thoughts, which in turn, will reduce your quality of life.

Also, there is some relation between your mind and your outer environment. How and why is this still a mystery? However, people have increasingly become curious about it, especially since 'The Secret' wave. We will discuss more about this in the next chapter.

So, analyse whether there is dirt in your mind. Analyse whether there is poison in your mind. If you find them, simply remove them. With practice, you will truly understand what these dirt and poison are, and you will understand how they harm or fool you while you are trying to live a good life.

Also, the mind needs purification quite frequently. How often do we need to clean our minds? As often as we clean our body, as often as we feed our stomach. I am emphasising this again because I don't want you to be under the wrong pretext that you need to take care of your mind only once or rarely. No, it requires supervision quite often, and you must take care of it. It is the starting point of your overall existence and well-being.

Chapter 3
STUDY OF MIND USE

How to use the mind is far more important than understanding what the mind is. This is because delving too deeply into trying to understand the mind leads to a lot of confusion and often without any provable conclusion. So, we will keep our understanding of the mind to the basics—

- The mind is an invisible organ.
- The whereabouts of the mind are not conclusively known.
- The mind is like the software and CPU of our existence and quality of life—it helps us think, guides us, and arranges fortune for us by placing opportunities and coincidences in our path. We simply need to develop an understanding of the relationship between mind and matter.
- The mind somehow converts our thinking into reality when we work with it, take proper actions, and understand the signals it sends via unexplainable experiences.

We are grateful to the 'The Secret' wave, which ignited interest in the relationship between 'mind and matter' and 'how thinking transforms our lives'. 'The Secret' was a book and a movie that propagated the knowledge that—

- A good mood is essential to attract positive things in life (just like what we discussed in the last chapter about Sant Tukaram: "Mann Kara Re Prasanna, Sarva Siddhiche Kaaran").
- The mind is like a magnet; what you think, you attract.
- It talks about the law of attraction: you are constantly—knowingly and unknowingly—attracting stuff and situations into your life. So, it's better to watch your mind and attract desirable matters and situations.

But the cause for concern is that when the concepts presented in the book are not well interpreted, it gives the impression that the knowledge is some sort of magic. People tend to misinterpret that we simply need to think about something, and we will get it. It is not like that. Anyway, let us move on to our topic.

Studying the mind and its relation with reality is not new. For ages, many philosophers, teachers, and gurus have imparted their wisdom on the topic. For example, the most profound knowledge about the mind was given by Lord Buddha.

"What you think, you become"

As simple as that, as plain as that, as raw as that. This wisdom, in my opinion, is the truth. Another version was provided by Mr. Henry Ford: "Whether you think you can, or you think you can't—you're right."

At different times, there were different books, such as—

- 'Power of Subconscious Mind' by Joseph Murphy.
- 'Magic of Thinking Big' by David J. Schwartz.
- 'Think and Grow Rich' by Napoleon Hill.
- 'The Power of Now' by Eckhart Tolle.
- 'Deep Work: Rules for Focused Success in a Distracted World' by Cal Newport.
- 'Conversations with God', a series of books written by Neale Donald Walsch.
- 'The Laws of the Spirit World' by Khorshed Bhavnagri.

The list is long, and various authors have presented their knowledge and their own analyses, which have been helpful and life-changing. I recommend reading some of them to enhance your life.

The state of your mind is the state of your external environment and not the other way around. Please understand this. Your external environment modifies itself as you modify your internal environment. This may not happen instantly. And the environment I am talking about here is not the physical environment but life situations, opportunities, friends, colleagues, job environment, gifts from fate, etc.

As Osho has said, "The whole world is nothing but a mirror."

The first step towards improving the state of mind is by purifying the mind, which we discussed in the previous chapter. Now, let us understand the importance of positive thinking.

The mind is like a garden; thoughts and mindsets are like seeds; and results are like plants or weeds. If left unattended, anything will grow over the mind. Those plants and weeds may or may not be desirable. But if you nurture your garden, replace unwanted plants with desirable ones, and sow beneficial seeds, then, with the given resources, you will have a planned and likeable garden.

'Yes Man' is a comedy film starring Jim Carrey, who decides to say 'yes' to every opportunity that comes his way, leading to unexpected adventures and personal growth. Positive thinking involves embracing such opportunities and saying 'yes' to life.

We are too small and insignificant to understand what life holds for us, but if we remain open to those gifts, then life can be magnificent and quite an adventure.

I have developed a technique to help us understand how to think in a particular situation. In this technique, think from the perspective of another character—a better character who is put in a similar situation and has come out victorious. We try to think about what must be going on in his mind and what thoughts he might be generating.

The beauty of this technique is that you can think of any identity or character. He can be a good person, a sportsperson, a successful businessman, an army leader, an exam topper, a top bodybuilder, a great actor, a great singer, a great doctor, etc. What must be the thoughts in the minds of great people? What are their thoughts in different situations?

We try to project what his inner mind must be when he is faced with such a situation and analyse the difference in thoughts. This process helps us get the right direction and is a hand-holding exercise in developing the skill of 'how to think'.

Let us take the example of a top sportsperson. What must be in his mind? Let us study the dominant thoughts and mindset of sportspersons:

1. Today, I will do more than yesterday.
2. I will bring out the beast in me.
3. I am doing my practice with full focus and dedication.
4. I will gradually improve my game.
5. I have to win only today's battle. This will strengthen me further to win tomorrow's battles.

Let us study the dominant thoughts and mindsets of exam toppers:

1. I will do it. Period.
2. I will improve every day until the exam day.
3. I will grab this opportunity no matter what.
4. Let's up the game. I will prepare for tough tests. Test me in all possible ways, in the toughest ways, and I will be ready.
5. Things may get harder, but remember, I have to do it.

Let us study the dominant thoughts and mindsets of powerful people:

1. Success is the most important ingredient of power.
2. This is not enough; I will do more, be more.
3. I have to win at any cost; success is the only option.
4. I am ready to work harder to complete the task.
5. I have to prepare in advance to remain ahead.

Let us study the dominant thoughts and mindsets of adventurers, the ones who followed their dreams:

1. I have to build myself to do this task.
2. I will have to take small steps to achieve big targets.
3. I have to experience the fight, the journey, the glory, and the risks.
4. Life lies in the unknown.
5. I believe in my dream.

Let us study the dominant thoughts and mindsets of the person who seeks peace:

1. Let me devise a system where I can remain off the grid.
2. Let me read this book this coming week.
3. I will secretly maintain my discipline.
4. I have to prepare for provisions and contingencies.

5. Let me do self-analysis and indulge in self-development.

Let us study the dominant thoughts and mindsets of intelligent people:

1. I have to learn this.
2. I have to become more intelligent; I have to think out of the box.
3. I have to challenge myself to be better.
4. I must not remain behind; let me understand the latest trends.
5. I have to develop something that will become the trend.

These are just predictions. Exact thoughts may differ, but we can be sure that 80-90% of dominant thoughts and mindsets will align with these lines.

Now analyse: what are your dominant thoughts, and how do your dominant thoughts and mindsets differ from these? Taking this reality check is a good starting point for bringing about positive transformations.

More Thought Research

The idea of 'Thought Control' has often been equated with 'Thought Restrictions', which has made it a confusing, impractical, and difficult concept to practice. Due to this interpretation, people lose interest in the practice of 'Thought Control'. Instead, a new way to understand the correct procedure is 'Thought Channelization'.

I will list some important questions that can help one generate useful thoughts for oneself. One may find some of these questions useful in the quest for self-discovery:

Important questions that give direction to the mind:

1. What can I do to be more successful?
2. How can I use my time more effectively?
3. What steps can I take to improve my life?
4. How can I become more attractive and beautiful?
5. What changes can I make to lead a healthier lifestyle?
6. How can I be more significant?
7. How can I become happier?
8. How can I make others happy?
9. What can I do to become rich?
10. How can society be improved?
11. What can be done to improve the current situation?

12. What strategies can help reduce anger?
13. How can anxiety be lessened?
14. What measures can reduce fear?
15. How can I enhance love, trust, and bonding within my family and relationships?
16. What can I do for the benefit of my family?
17. How can I contribute positively to the organisation I work for?
18. What can I do to enhance societal conditions?
19. How can I contribute to the betterment of my nation?
20. What steps can I take to boost my self-confidence?
21. How can I increase my personal value?
22. What can I do to enhance the value of my family and organisation?
23. What can I do to become great?
24. What should I do to undertake significant work?
25. How can I cultivate big thinking?
26. What actions can I take to complete a major project or work?
27. How can I improve the quality of my thoughts?
28. What should I do to create a fortune?

29. What actions can I take to advance my goals?
30. In which direction do I want my thoughts to go?

I am pretty sure that most of us do not typically think in this direction. Pondering over some of the above-mentioned questions once in a while will help us gain a better direction in our thinking.

Think of a weighing scale. If you place a grain of sand in one of the trays, it probably won't make much difference to the balance of the scale. But if you add another grain, and another, and another, then eventually the scale will begin to tilt in that direction. Your thoughts work in the same way; if you have enough of one particular type of thought, it will affect your quality of life and your overall being.

Now, I am going to introduce some more concepts. Gradually, I will increase the complexity of these concepts, and the reader may skip the rest of the chapter if she does not agree with the ideas presented.

Some ideas:

- A new life does not start with a new date, a new location, a new job, or new people. It starts with a new mind. If you change your mind, your life changes. This way, you can restart your life at any age and in any place.

- Self-development is not dependent on the external environment. You cannot use the excuse that because of this or that, you could not achieve something. Throughout history, the world has seen examples where people have achieved great feats under the most adverse conditions. The point is not to compare people's journeys, but to get inspired by such extraordinary people and prove that with genuine will and effort, one can progress under any condition.
- A positive mindset is our true friend. It provides solutions and encouragement. It can help us become what we have never been and do what we have never done.
- What we believe we lack ends up defining what we love. The brain only craves what it lacks. This is part of Maya, the illusion, which we discussed in the chapter 'Negativity in the present world'. Once you achieve success and can have everything you think of, you will lose interest in that stuff. At that stage, you will crave simplicity and seclusion. This is how it is, and it is a complex phenomenon.
- Your mind will provide evidence for any belief that you hold. Understand this: if you

say something is good, your mind will give you reasons for that thing to be good; on the contrary, if you say the same exact thing is bad, your mind will provide evidence of that, confirming the belief that it is bad.

- Time, life, and the external environment will deteriorate our minds if we don't protect and nourish them. As simple as that. Recognise this.

A positive mindset is the only thing that increases the possibility of achieving wealth and happiness in life and the afterlife. Yes, I said afterlife, too. This is a very hard-to-accept concept for many, and I have discussed the afterlife in later chapters. But let me explain the point. We have discussed in detail the importance of positive thinking while living. It is the practice that helps us remain in a good mood and increases our chances of success. If positive thinking can become a habit, then nothing is better than that. It becomes our integral part. The afterlife is only slightly different from the life that we are aware of on Earth, with only some changes in material content. If positive thinking becomes an integral part, then we can carry that essence into our afterlife and benefit from it. More is discussed in the later chapters.

Language constraints and mind

Become calm and observe your mind. As you read, you can hear your voice inside your head. The thoughts that you generate are made of the vocabulary that is known to you. Let this clarity sink in. You cannot think beyond your known vocabulary and language. This means that our thought generation capacity is capped by, and constrained by, the known language and vocabulary.

That is why, if you need to improve your thoughts, then you may need better language and a better vocabulary. Or, until then, let us continue studying about the mind.

Observer – A Complicated Analysis

I present the last of the complicated ideas. It is the most complex analysis. If the reader cannot relate to this, then she can skip this part and jump to the next chapter.

Do you want to know who you really are?

In the movie 'Peaceful Warrior', one piece of wisdom is that we are not our minds. The truth is that we are only part of the mind. Or rather, the mind is merely one part of us.

Let me tell you how I got to know that I am not my mind. It's through experiments and close analysis that I understood that our mind is simply a small part of our being.

Say hello inside your mind. Close your eyes and repeat the process. Now, analyse who said hello and who listened. Pay attention and say hello again to observe better. In my analysis, the inside of the mind is like a closed room. The entity which said hello is me, located at the centre of the room. The listener or observer is like the walls of the closed room, also me, who merely listened.

Now, say something more than "hello" inside your mind and continue observing. For example, engage in self-talk. Know that you are generating the thoughts.

Until awareness has grown to the level of separating the 'observer' from the 'mind', we keep identifying ourselves with our mind, which is faulty and prone to illusions.

The observer part of the mind—the wall—simply observes. Whenever a thought is generated, the awareness of 'who is observing that thought' helps in realising there are separate entities: the observer and the mind.

The observer is completely silent and non-reactive.

When I associate myself with the Observer rather than the mind (which generates the thoughts), I realise the following—

- With small meditation, I can truly calm my mind.
- I realise that my mind is altogether a separate entity if I identify myself with the Observer within.
- Understanding the mind's reaction pattern becomes easy when we are with the Observer.
- How the mind creates 'stuff/drama' for itself.
- The scam of the word 'I' – what is really I?
- How the mind is keeping 'awareness' trapped!

Being with observer

The realisation that 'there is an observer' inside "me" and it is different from the mind has been a revolutionary one. This is prime knowledge; probably what ancient wisdom called 'Atmagyan'.

This experiment has been successful and life-transforming. 'The observer' exposes the true nature of the mind. And this helps in affirming that 'whatever is, is correct and just'.

As there are two entities inside me, it becomes clear to understand the nature of the mind as well as the nature of the observer.

With practice, one can spot the observer with any thought (rather than the initial 'hello' we used).

Try to understand the concept of the observer to understand the drama of the world.

Having understood the concept of an observer, one can bring the value of any thought to zero. This is, in a way, enlightenment. Bringing down the value of any thoughts will be through wisdom and not by ego or deliberate attempt. You will simply lose interest in generating any thought as you will fall in love with the silence of the observer within.

Be with the observer, and this is true liberation.

The observer doesn't say anything because nothing is to be said, and there is no point in saying anything.

Section 3: The Life

Chapter 4
ANALYSIS OF LIFE

If one is low on self-awareness and doesn't study life, then he keeps on doing random stuff. Meaning in life comes if we do self-analysis and life analysis. With a little effort, we can make living a good experience, which otherwise simply goes on.

We exist. We simply exist. We may not have chosen it. But now what? You cannot complain that 'why do I exist?' Such complaining will not yield any results either. Instead, try to make something better of it.

Once in a while, we need to think about where we are, where we want to go, whether we are taking the necessary steps to get there, whether we are enjoying the adventure of life, and what improvements we need for our mindset.

"An unexamined life is not worth living," said Socrates. So, examine life. What is this living and existing? What is to be done? No one knows for certain. But we get ideas from learning from different people, people from different times, their stories, etc. We will understand that people who have lived with passion, followed their dreams, introspected, tried to do something new, tried to make a connection with God, and sought guidance from Him have generally lived meaningful lives.

My analysis of life is that we need to strive to improve our lives. This should become a habit, a mindset. Life is different for everyone; everyone is in different circumstances and raised in different situations. So, whatever your situation may be, good or bad, try to improve it further.

Life gets harder in the next phase

While living your life, you will often be given false hope that once you clear your 10th standard, life will get easier; once you clear your 12th standard, life will be easier; once you graduate, life will become easier; once you get a job, and so on. The truth is that life becomes a little harder with each passing phase.

Harder in the sense that you will face more challenges, dynamic challenges for which you have not been trained yet. Life becomes interdependent on many aspects, and to get things done, you will have to push a little more, manage a little more, think out of the box, make extra efforts, etc.

I don't want to say that life becomes utterly disappointing. No. With each new phase, life also becomes beautiful. You gain experience, wealth, freedom, and respect too. But this happens only if you satisfactorily succeed in earlier phases.

So, the point is to train yourself hard. Don't expect life to keep getting easier. Instead, assume that it's going to get tougher and use this idea to train harder. This approach will ease your journey by making you stronger than the upcoming challenges. So be ready, build yourself. Hence, the saying goes, "Life doesn't get easier; you just get stronger."

Life is unpredictable, yes, though not 100%

We think only from our limited perspectives. We do not know who can achieve what. We do not know what someone is capable of. We do not know how much time one has on Earth. The same applies to you; you do not know what you will achieve or what you may become. But what is certain is that you will not become anything if you don't try sincerely. As the saying goes, you will definitely miss the shot that you don't take. But if you aim for something and don't hit, then that's also fine. Again, as the saying goes, aim for the moon, and you will at least be among the stars. These two quotes define the complex scenario of life well.

So, life may be unpredictable, but we also have just enough control over it. You will learn more about how to go about it in subsequent chapters. But to explain in a nutshell, the mantra is: choose the goal and work towards it with devotion (to the level of obsession). You will achieve something good and become better.

Now vs 'whole lifetime'

This is very beautiful knowledge. Now is the only true time where you can solve your worries on the mental plane. Now is the only true time where you can sort your thoughts and motivate yourself. Now is the only true time when you can communicate with God.

Now is the only true time. Now is the truth. Now is real; the rest is illusory.

Now is the time when you can change the direction of your life. And if we are aware of it, now is also the gift.

'The Power of Now: A Guide to Spiritual Enlightenment' is a book by Eckhart Tolle that decodes the power of Now. Try to inculcate the practice of remaining in the present every now and then.

Tomorrow is an illusion, but today is reality. Try to make today a little better. Have an 'improving today' oriented mindset.

Today is limited but true. Tomorrow is unlimited, but it's an illusion.

Fight to make today better.

We always work for a better tomorrow. But when it comes, instead of enjoying it, we again think of a better tomorrow! Let us have a better today.

This is important learning. Today is the most important day of all.

Today is a special day, not because it won't come again, but because it's real.

Today I can practice. I can practice being brave, bold, expressive, real, knowing reality, and being visionary.

At this point, let us recall the teaching of Master Oogway from the movie 'Kung Fu Panda': "Yesterday is history, tomorrow is a mystery, but today is a gift. That is why it is called the present."

Understanding Karma

The theory of karma is life-transforming wisdom. Karma means deeds or actions. Whatever you do, good or bad, will be returned to you.

Now, the definition, though plain, does not have a shallow meaning. Having understood the karma theory on the surface, one cannot strategise good fortune just by deliberately doing some good. That is, if you want something good to happen to you and hence you do good for others, it will not work that way. It is then a matter of intention. Intentions have to be genuine.

If we believe in Reincarnation

Many spiritual scriptures have stressed on 'Reincarnation'. Reincarnation means taking birth again and again. For analysis purposes, if we believe that the theory of reincarnation is true, then our priorities and values may change.

If we believe that reincarnation is real, then it means that we have taken many births. In the present life, you are what you know you are. But in previous lives, you might have been something that you never knew. The journey of birth and death has been rather endless. It goes back to unimaginable history. Who knows what you have achieved or suffered in all those lives?

This cycle of birth and death is endless. This idea expands our minds. If my existence is endless, represented in the form of birth and death, then what really matters? Everything we consider great has no meaning, every judgement we hold for others is silly, pride in our ideas or achievements is empty, and every feeling that we felt or will feel is not an astonishment. We existed 10,000 years ago, and we will exist for another 10,000 years too. Much before most religions came into existence and much later, humans have explored all possible truths.

So, what is the point? Probably, the point is not to give much importance to birth and death. Probably, the point is to remember the meaning of this theory of reincarnation and not to fear death or rebirth while living and making choices. Maybe the point is to live in the present moment and improve continuously. Maybe the important thing is to live fully or, as Osho has said, live dangerously. Probably, what matters is how we live.

Existence is our prison

Many people find solace in the idea that death is the end and that living or existing will end at death. But many spiritual and religious scriptures have talked about the afterlife and existence beyond death. Now, there is no scientific proof of the afterlife; there just cannot be. But for the sake of research and to understand the perspective of so many books, let us just assume that the afterlife exists.

This would mean that we exist, and death is not the end. We will exist forever. It is just that our time on Earth is limited, but our being remains what it is. The habits we formed, the karma we accumulated, and the knowledge and wisdom we gained remain with us, with our souls, even in the afterlife. It is just that memory is lost, but we remain 'we'.

The afterlife will not be a sudden change from the life we are living. There will be only slight modifications, and the journey continues.

This way, our existence is merely a prison. There is no escape. So, our only option is to focus on ourselves and develop throughout.

We have discussed similar ideas in detail in a later chapter, too.

Wisdom by Albert Camus

To understand the wisdom provided by Mr. Camus, let us study the story of Sisyphus. Sisyphus, a figure from Greek mythology, was condemned to repeat forever the same meaningless task of pushing a boulder up a mountain, only to see it roll down again just as it neared the top. This was his punishment by the gods. A common understanding is that he must be suffering to perform that meaningless task again and again.

But Mr. Camus offers a different perspective. He urged us to imagine Sisyphus happy. Camus claims that when Sisyphus acknowledges the futility of his task and the certainty of his fate, he is freed to realise the absurdity of his situation and hence reaches a state of contented acceptance.

The story of Sisyphus is an analogy for our existence. Living or existing is absurd because we do not know why we are here, how long we will be here, and what to do.

Camus presents Sisyphus's ceaseless and pointless toil as a metaphor for modern lives spent working at futile jobs in factories and offices. "The workman of today works every day in his life at the same tasks, and this fate is no less absurd. But it is tragic only at the rare moments when he becomes conscious of it."

But we have to work, and if we game the system and find our little happiness in achievements that we achieve or devote our attention to mastering the work, focusing on self-development and life development, then we can bear the suffering caused by the idea that 'life is absurd'.

In your head, you say between three hundred and a thousand words every minute to yourself. Those words can be positive (I can do it) or negative (Oh god, I can't take this anymore). It turns out that when these words are positive, they have a huge effect on your mental toughness and your ability to keep going. Subsequent studies of military personnel back this up.

Optimists told themselves a story that may not have been true, but it kept them going, often allowing them to beat the odds. Psychologist Shelley Taylor says that "a healthy mind tells itself flattering lies." The pessimists were more accurate and realistic, and they ended up depressed. The truth can hurt.

Life is not the same for everyone

Life can be unfair to some. It does not treat everyone in a similar way. It is harsh on some while it favours others. Why is it like this? It is not known. It is just like that. In whatever manner life may be treating you, hang on, purify your mind and install a positive mindset by taking the help of 'positive thoughts and mindset of the person who could have changed his life in similar situations' as discussed in the previous chapter. This will help.

Chapter 5

PURPOSES OF LIFE – THINGS THAT MATTER IN LIFE

Since the start of the book, I have been talking about 'things that matter' in life. Things that matter in life are also the purposes of life. I use the plural word 'purposes' and not the singular word 'purpose', because in my observation there may not be a single purpose of life. Often, you may wonder what might be the purpose of life? From my experience and the books that I have read, I will list down the purposes of life. These purposes are not in order of priority, but rather just a consolidated list.

I have broadly listed seven purposes of life. These are the things that matter in life. We have expanded on the following ideas in different parts of the book.

1. **Purpose of life concerning mind and its training:**

   - Studying, analysing, and improving the mind are among the purposes of life. This is a never-ending process and you will find real joy in this endeavour. We have discussed this in another chapter. Thinking, analysing, reading about the mind, and understanding its power are very interesting and lead us to the right path. This exercise also brings us closer to the truth.

- Additionally, continuously training the mind to develop certain mindsets or attitudes can also be considered one of the purposes of life. Mindsets such as identifying opportunities in adversity, not complaining, finding solutions, moving forward, removing dirt and poison from the mind from time to time, and being ready to work in every situation are critical.
- Learning the skill of 'Purification of the mind' is one of the purposes of life, as discussed in the chapter 'Mind Purification'. You must learn how to purify the mind by changing dirt or poison into purity. There is no escape from learning this skill. Unless your mind becomes purer, you won't be at peace, nor will there be any real satisfaction in life. Developing the ability to purify the mind is also a kind of test. You will fail in life (and the afterlife too) if you cannot develop the ability to purify the

mind. Bad things will happen, and bad situations will arise, and the mind will definitely get temporarily impure. There will be anger, bitterness, curses, and complaints, but then you, and only you, have to protect yourself. So, develop the ability to purify the mind and practice it forever.

2. **Purpose of life concerning acceptance:**

    - Accept the situation you are in. Analyse it and plan to improve the situation. Whether you are rich or poor, successful or not yet successful, have certain health problems, or feel lost in life, simply accept it and set a more desirable and enriching goal, and work towards it. As Osho has said, "Whatever there is in life, accept it, know it, and live it. From this acceptance will come the transformation."

    - Feeling gratitude is also one of the purposes of life. Saying thank you to your luck, God, or an unknown force (whatever you want to call it) is necessary to release a sigh of relief. Practising gratitude often is one of the purposes of life. I will tell you one thing: it is not that we have to be grateful only for the good things in life, but even the challenges faced and difficult times in life need to be thanked.

They give a unique flavour to our lives and help us in developing ourselves.

3. **Purpose of life concerning 'way of living' and success:**

- One of the purposes of life is to 'live the adventure'. Unpredictable, unplanned events can occur in life and the afterlife. You must develop a mindset that you will persevere through it. No matter how challenging the situation may be, you can certainly enjoy the process of solving the problems at hand. So, embrace the adventure.
- To be successful, or to strive sincerely for it, is another purpose of life. Wealth, power, position, influence, dominance, skills, knowledge, etc., are prime elements of success. We find these elements in every field: from sportspersons to writers, from singers to comedians, from businessmen to government officers, from scientists to doctors. We will find successful people, with the above-mentioned elements, in every field. In my opinion, we need at least 2-3 massive successes in life to lead a good life.
- Another purpose of life is to learn to do things with intensity and by giving 100% of your being. I will introduce a useful

question here: Whatever small or big, short-term or long-term goal you want to achieve, just ask yourself, what does it mean to give 100% to achieve that goal? The answers that will flow to your mind will astonish you. Then check if you can live up to that level of obsession. Some obsessions are good, for example, achieving a certain level of fitness or acquiring a particular skill that will aid your career or hobby. In general, you will receive answers like strict discipline, restricted use of mobile and social media, strong commitment, etc. So, analyse what constitutes giving 100%. Make your own list of dos and don'ts that would mean giving 100%. And try to adhere to those standards. You will love the journey. You may or may not achieve the desired results but you will transform into a better person.

- Learning to live a secret life is also one of the purposes of life. In today's connected world, driven by social media, living a secret life has its own value. Don't let anyone know what you are up to. Let them think what they want. Keep your thoughts and plans to yourself. Keep working on them. And don't declare them unless they are completely ready.

Learning to live such a secret life is a purpose of life.

4. **Purpose of life concerning health**

   - Being healthy, inculcating healthy habits, and taking care of your body are very important. This is real wealth. Maintaining good health is one of the purposes of life. There is an entire science behind building good health. In a nutshell, one must exercise and consume five nutrients: fat, vitamins, protein, carbohydrates, and minerals. One must drink plenty of water and include fibre in their diet. It is also necessary to ensure sound sleep. And finally, one must maintain a good mood.

5. **The purpose of life is to sharpen the saw.**

   - One of the purposes of life is to regularly remember and revisit certain knowledge, plans, goals, and standards. Please remember that you cannot become great without recalling these. You will realise that forgetting is so natural and swift, and it is one of the main culprits in our lives which results in a state of directionlessness. We forget what we want, what we should achieve, our path, what matters, etc. We either forget everything or get distracted in this world. When we forget these important things, our life goes haywire. And only when we remember these, do we come back to life. So please, maintain a diary, preferably a digital diary, and write things that are important to you—like what you want to experience, what you want to achieve, what you want to be, by when, action plans, prayers, your conversations with God, etc. The list is endless. Keep this diary fairly secret and revisit it often to remain on track.

6. **Purpose of life concerning karma or work:**

   - One of the purposes of life is to do a lot of work. Train yourself and practice continuously to work more and faster. Greatness is not found in the results or at the end of the journey; rather, it exists in everyday work. The more work you do, the more experience and advantage you will gain. The more you will learn. And if you develop the habit of starting work early, you will have some time for yourself after completing your tasks. These small 'earned times' will make a significant difference over a long period; for example, you will be able to spend more time with family, pursue a hobby, work on a project that interests you, or go for an adventure.

7. **Purpose of life concerning spirituality.**

   - One of the purposes of life is to understand God. I came across the concept of'Conversations with God'in the book and YouTube movie 'Conversations with God' by Neale Donald Walsch. These are beautiful works. We need to establish a conversation with God and seek guidance from Him. I am not talking about rituals or superficial practices, but about your secret and deep connection with God.

Chapter 6
HOW TO IMPROVE LIFE?

The first thing needed to improve life is the will to do so. Where there is a will, there is a way. Of course, each one of us is in different situations and life does not treat everyone equally. Despite that, the struggle is the same for everyone who wants to improve their lives. This struggle will sometimes break you; it will get difficult, with failures after failures, and one may lose hope. This is a normal process. But we have got no choice but to move forward.

When things are hard, what can you really do? Finding solutions is the only real option. Miracles happen when you are determined to improve your life, when you are determined to achieve something.

At this point, I would like to bring your attention to the YouTube channel of Ben Lionel Scott. I personally find his videos life-transforming and nearer to the truth. Give it a try.

Dilemma of preacher

What is happening in this book is that I am sharing some life advice with you. This is a sort of preaching of life knowledge. Often, readers might think, if he is giving such knowledge, why is he not very successful himself?

This is the dilemma of a preacher. If he wants to share some good advice, then critics (rightly so) will ask, "What is your credibility for providing life-transforming knowledge? And have you yourself applied it in your life?"

This scrutiny is a good trend. The one who is giving Gyan (life-transforming knowledge) should be scrutinized by readers. The preacher should have some credibility and achievements in his kitty before guiding others. And I urge every reader and student of life to verify the authenticity of a preacher; otherwise, some influential preachers, without substantial credibility, may misguide you. That would be hypocrisy. So, beware.

Also, preachers are often seen as perfect people. After all, if he is giving life-transforming knowledge, then he must be perfect and without any fault. But NO. Preachers are also normal people like you, who simply have experienced something and are sharing their knowledge with you. They can also be wrong at times.

Having said that, I have provided information about me in last section of the book.

The good thing about 'improving life' is that it is a never-ending process, and each next achievement gives a sense of fulfillment. Clearly speaking, improving life has a direct relation with improving the mind and taking actions on time, or preferably before time. People who have absolutely killed procrastination and laziness from their lives generally lead a much better life. So, let us start this chapter with killing laziness and procrastination'

Time is much shorter than it appears. We have expanded on this idea in subsequent paragraphs.

So, be prompt and complete your work before time and remain (mentally) burden-free. Laziness and procrastination are not worth it. Laziness and procrastination make life dull, causing you to sacrifice many opportunities. Also, to be lazy is to be weak.

Refer to the discourse on karma mentioned in this chapter.

I have come to understand that 'Intelligence' is very necessary to improve life and live a good and fulfilling life. Intelligence is the ability to understand

and decode hidden meanings, plan and predict the required time for certain tasks, solve problems, think out of the box, be ambitious, have love for wisdom, and relate to people and situations. These traits of intelligence are not exhaustive.

It is not that the level of intelligence is fixed at birth. I am of the opinion that intelligence can be improved; one just needs to have a strong will for it. Improving intelligence is a part of self-development. If one sincerely works to improve intelligence, then increasing the level of intelligence is possible. Activities such as studying, solving puzzles, problem-solving, analysing, and engaging in creative work can help increase intelligence.

At this point in time, I would like to discuss Lord Ganesha. Lord Ganesha is the God of intelligence and wisdom (God of Sadd Vivek Buddhi). "Sadd Vivek Buddhi" is a phrase in Sanskrit, an ancient language of India, which translates to "pure, discriminative intellect" in English. Each word in the phrase carries significance: 'Sadd' means pure or true, 'Vivek' refers to discrimination or discernment, and 'Buddhi' denotes intellect or the faculty of reasoning and understanding. Together, "Sadd Vivek Buddhi" refers to a state of having a pure, discerning intellect capable of making wise decisions and discerning truth from falsehood. It is often used in philosophical and spiritual contexts to emphasise the importance of cultivating clear and discerning thinking.

My urge to the reader is that she should focus on improving intelligence. As discussed in one of the previous chapters about negativity in the world, the environment is somehow not conducive to improving your intelligence. You have to protect yourself and improve your intelligence.

Let us read about Walson's Law: If you put knowledge and intelligence first at all times, then money keeps coming in.

For a certain period, we may become purposeless and directionless when we do not acquire any specific mindset or identity or work towards certain goals or thoughts. That is our condition. Without a particular mindset, we are lost, directionless, and slowly drift into inactivity and irrelevance. I have learnt and relearnt this many times. The conclusion is that we must choose certain identities or mindsets which we like and are necessary for us in given situations, and learn from that mindset to get direction, purpose, and joy in life.

For example, for a certain period during a long vacation, I decided to relax and be lazy. I did that and enjoyed it for some time. Then, after a few days, my mind became blank, I was living without any sense of direction or purpose. I felt that I was relaxing too much and needed to do something. This is the catch: when we decide not to have any goal or certain mindset, we simply drift away into inactivity and irrelevance. This example from a long vacation and the choice to be lazy highlights how an absence of a defined goal or mindset can result in a blank and directionless state of mind. But then I started studying my mind. There was nothing substantial in it at that time. So, I had to acquire certain identities to get in touch with the desired mindset. I chose identities such as 'that who is health-conscious', 'that who is writing a book', and 'that who is living peacefully and happily'. Here, I started getting ideas, and I started enjoying life.

The learning is, in a given situation, choose your identities. Consider this – 'That (person) who is... (choose your pick)' and try to analyse his/her mind. You can have more than one identity to follow to fulfill you. Learn from those mindsets, and get directions. The idea is to learn from these chosen mindsets, gaining insights and directions that can lead to a more fulfilling life. Hence, engage in self-reflection and consciously choose identities or mindsets that align with our goals and desires. We have discussed in detail about possible mindsets of many such identities in other chapters of this book.

Understanding Karmas

When we hear about karma, we usually think only of 'Good Karma' and 'Bad Karma'. We associate karma with heaven and hell and recall the famous wisdom of Lord Krishna, "Karmanye Vadhikaraste, Ma phaleshou Kada chana — You have the right to perform your actions, but you are not entitled to the fruits of the actions. Ma Karma Phala Hetur Bhurmatey Sangostva Akarmani — Do not let the fruit be the purpose of your actions, and therefore you won't be attached to not doing your duty."

Karma is the truth. It's like a law: what you do, you get. It emphasises on action.

However, in my opinion, karma may not only be classified as 'good' or 'bad'. Karma can be categorised as follows:

- Useful karma.
- Life-building karma.
- Health-building karma.
- Money-growing karma.
- Happiness-increasing karma.
- Karma that places you in better situations, etc.

Now, you may say these categories of karma are intended to achieve certain goals. Yes, but while these channelized karmas increase our chances of achieving the goal, what will truly be in our fate remains a mystery. However, when we engage in these channelized karmas, we achieve something that elevates our present standing. This is akin to the saying, "Aim for the moon, if you miss you may land among the stars."

The karma theory states, "As you sow, so shall you reap." This is just one side of the story. Yes, karma will have consequences, but what if we don't act? Will there be no consequences? From my observation, the answer is no. If you don't act, the result is not 'no consequences', but rather 'more troubles'.

Thus, if you act, there will be consequences/ results. But if you don't act, you will face troubles. Therefore, the conclusion is that you must engage in karma—anyhow.

Why is it necessary to do a lot of work, and to do it early?

Here's the thing: you have to do the work anyhow. If you do work today, it will directly or indirectly benefit you tomorrow. And if you don't do work today, it will directly or indirectly trouble you tomorrow. It's simple.

The benefit or trouble can manifest in the form of—

- Getting or losing extra time to do other personal activities.
- Gaining or losing goodwill.
- Moving ahead vs getting stuck in the same old task.

So, do a lot of work a lot early and remain free from the bonding of unfinished tasks.

Time is faster than you think.

Convex mirrors on the outside of cars often contain a message that says something like, "Objects in mirror are closer than they appear." This means that the objects (rear vehicles) appear farther away but in reality, they are closer than they appear. This is also an important mantra of life. Every adversity in life is closer than it appears. Death, losses, diseases, losing loved ones, and bad times are closer than they appear. It is a bitter truth, but understanding this concept will help you prioritize what truly matters in life.

Time moves faster than you think. The moment you wake up, within 2-3 hours, your day may seem to be over due to your already occupied schedule or tasks or the job. This happens every day. Many people don't realise this, but the frustration of not having time for themselves accumulates over time. Don't be like them. Develop yourself to be ready before time. In the present fast-moving world, you must earn time for yourself by disciplining yourself.

- Rise before it's too late.
- Get it done before it's too late.
- Get disciplined before it's too late.

- Get healthy before it's too late.
- Read before it's too late.
- Learn before it's too late.
- Finish the work before it's too late.

There are many benefits of doing things in advance or as per planning. First of all, you will have time for yourself wherein you won't worry about the tasks during that time. Second, your work will get done because it's easy to do 95% of the work, but it's difficult to complete 100% of it. However, if you develop yourself to be ready before time, you will be among those who complete their work ahead of schedule. Third, the rewards, which can't be anticipated. Direct and indirect rewards, tangible and intangible, will follow you when the world knows that you finish work before time.

Story of Drops and Cuts

Among various stories that I have developed, this is one of my favourite stories. In this story, a drop is a drop of water and a cut is a small cut on our skin.

The two associated phrases of drops and cuts are–

1. The Ocean is made up of Drops.
2. Death by a Thousand Cuts.

A drop is an insignificant component of the ocean. The ocean is the most visible and noticeable part. Similarly, Death is also a significant and noticeable event, whereas a small cut on the skin is negligible.

People get awestruck by the view of the mighty ocean and get absolutely fearful and hopeless in the face of death.

But know one thing, and this is the truth as well: the ocean is made up of drops, and death is not sudden; it is an accumulation of thousands of cuts.

In our lives, we ignore the drops and cuts while noticing only the oceans and deaths. And this is what makes the BIG DIFFERENCE. Drops are small and insignificant like good habits/efforts, whereas cuts are small yet correctible like bad habits/tendencies.

Let's look at the drops that we may ignore –

1. Getting up early.
2. Marginally building any skill.
3. Completing tasks on time, or even a bit early.
4. Brushing teeth twice daily.
5. Inculcating any small healthy habits, such as drinking enough water.
6. Doing at least 15 minutes of exercise daily.

Let's look at the cuts that we generally ignore –

1. Procrastination.

2. Justifying "only one cigarette" or a small drink.
3. Being just 5 minutes late.
4. Opting for "just one item" of fast food.
5. Saying "just not today, I will resume this tomorrow."

This is a general idea of drops and cuts. Greatness lies in every day, whereas results—whether great or terrible—happen only on a single fateful day. People notice only oceans and death. Don't do the same. I urge you to give utmost importance to everyday drops and cuts without worrying about the ocean or death.

I mentioned that one of the purposes of life is to be successful. Yes, it is very necessary to be successful. Now, there are many forms of success: small success, medium success, and massive-large successes. The general perception of success—wealth, position, power, abundance, good relationships, etc.—can generally be considered massive-large success. Other examples include being number one in the country or world, extraordinary influence (like the incident when footballer Cristiano Ronaldo removed two Coca-Cola bottles as he said 'Agua' (Portuguese for water), urging people to drink water instead and crashed Coca-Cola's shares by $4 billion), having so much success that you need bodyguards, etc. That is massive success. While small and medium successes include appreciation at the job, some trophies at a regional level, class toppers, getting a promotion, etc. I will say that massive successes are as important as small and medium successes.

There is an ideology and a group of people who will say that success is relative, achieving little is also a success, be content with what you have, no need to achieve more, etc. Let me tell you they are simply projecting their thoughts on you and they fear that you should not become more than them. Otherwise, they will be left alone. Stay away from people and ideologies that promote stagnancy and mediocrity, instead, never stop, never settle. Big and massive successes are the real deal, other successes will not truly bring fulfillment. Be on the path of achieving big success, while constantly achieving small and medium success. As I said earlier, never settle.

Another reference we come across in self-help books regarding improving life is improving our thinking. We have discussed the use of the mind and mindset development in different chapters, but let us explore some more relevant ideas here.

It is said that 'thoughts become things'. This may appear magical, but the relationship is not very direct or immediate. It simply means that if you have evolved your mind to the level where it constantly produces good, positive, solution-oriented thoughts and thoughts that evoke good feelings, then you will naturally become a problem-solver and an enthusiastic person. Consequently, wealth and abundance will follow.

Another reference to this idea is 'Shabdo se jiwan banata hai' (words make your life), suggesting that by choosing encouraging and positive words for your life, those words will indirectly improve your life. Thoughts are the single most effective entities to build an extraordinary life. Thoughts are everything; they either build up the mood or destroy it. If something is not right in life, it's because of wrong thoughts. If something is right in life, it's because of right thoughts.

Some scientists explain this phenomenon with the example of energy. Thoughts are vibrations and possess a certain level of energy. The following text delves into metaphysical and philosophical discussions. Life situations, fortune or misfortunes, and all good and bad things are also forms of energy with specific frequencies. The principle here is that one frequency will attract another of the same frequency, a concept known as synchronization or harmony. Synchronization occurs when two or more oscillating systems adjust their rhythms to harmonize, often resulting in them oscillating in phase or at the same frequency.

If you consistently produce better frequencies, then situations, fortune, and guidance corresponding to those frequencies will manifest in your life. It's like a rule: good fortune, wisdom, and favourable situations have certain fixed frequencies. If you, through conscious effort, generate these frequencies, then those elements will appear in your life.

For example, someone might describe experiencing synchronicity when their thoughts or intentions align perfectly with events in their life, leading to a sense of meaningful coincidence. While these metaphysical and philosophical uses of synchronization may not involve literal oscillations or frequencies as in physical systems, they often convey the idea of alignment, harmony, or resonance.

Discipline

When you are disciplined, you get more time and quality time for both work and leisure. As simple as that. Those who do not plan or remain undisciplined end up burning their time and diminishing the quality of focus in both areas.

As I said earlier, life becomes tougher in each subsequent phase (and probably in the afterlife too, whether you will go to hell or heaven). In such situations, you must be disciplined to find solutions and achieve more. Discipline allows you to provide quality attention to your health, other ventures, and work.

We need 0.30-1.00 hours of time for health; 1.00 hour for study or self-development; 2 hours with family; 7 hours of sleep; and 1-2 hours for daily chores. This totals around 13–14 hours. The remaining 10 hours are for work, school, or economy-related activities. This is a normal working day, but there are also many holidays and rest days.

Consider that if you are disciplined and rise one hour early, say at 4:30 or 5 am, you gain an extra hour each day. I am of the opinion that we need to get up early and go to bed early. This is a hard thing to do nowadays. But many disciplined and well-to-do people have been doing it since ages and gaining from it. One may find many counterarguments that it does not matter when you get up, where they quote a few exceptions of some successful people who get up late and work till late at night. These are tactics to influence and hinder progress, as discussed in the 'Negativity in the present world' chapter.

Also, remember that when you feel like giving up, someone else in the world, possibly in a similar situation and pursuing a similar goal, might still be persevering. Discipline plays a major role in this competitive world. Discipline and consistency are essential to prepare the mind for any goal. Willpower for discipline and consistency is the greatest differentiator.

Just be disciplined and manage your time well. You will lead a much better life. Once you start completing your work ahead of schedule through discipline, you will realise that you have more time for other activities. This is why I say real freedom lies in discipline. The more you seek freedom in ad-hocness or indiscipline, the more enslaved you become. Without discipline, you will always find yourself short of time for work and other activities, and you will compromise on quality.

Even when life becomes challenging, don't stop striving for something better. Let there be pain; it's okay. Maintain your discipline.

Those who are disciplined develop a more appealing, distinctive, and attractive personality and character over time. Being disciplined means being self-controlled too. In this distracted world where many choose to be undisciplined, winning has become easier. Keep this in mind.

Self-motivation and self-encouragement

As discussed in the first chapter, the world will discourage you and may not believe in you. You don't need the world to motivate and encourage you; it is your responsibility to self-motivate and self-encourage. Don't seek it anywhere else.

Self-encouragement and self-motivation involve self-talks that increase enthusiasm, courage, willpower, etc. Encourage yourself to achieve certain goals, to be ambitious, and to keep going. Say to yourself, "Yes, I have to do it, I can do it, I will push forward, I will remain silent till it is done."

Choose your adventure, determine where you wish to go, and work towards it. What's wrong with trying? Don't give excuses; it is your life, and you have to improve it.

If you keep doing what you've been doing, you'll keep getting what you've been getting. Hence, bring positive changes to your life. Build your dreams brick by brick.

Fear is often disguised as practicality. In one speech, Jim Carrey mentioned, "Fear is disguised as practicality." This means what we often consider practical can actually be our fears. And because we have accepted "practical ways of thinking", asking for what we really want seems impossibly out of reach and ridiculous to expect. That is why we never dare to ask the universe for it. But in the speech, he urges us to abandon fear, which is disguised as practicality, and to ask for the big things.

Positive obsession. Giving 100%

One question that will help you self-reflect is: "What does giving 100% mean for a certain task?" You might be in different phases of life. Some of you might be students, athletes, scientists, entrepreneurs, or developing something. Whatever category you are in, simply ask yourself what it means to give 100% to the goal you are working on. What will be the dos and don'ts when someone is giving 100%? What will be the sleeping rules, entertainment rules, and TV and internet rules when someone is giving 100%?

The answers will astonish you and provide the required guidance. They will also open up your mind and eyes, helping you understand what more or differently you can do.

These answers point towards obsession. In my opinion, obsession for beneficial/positive goals is a good thing. Positive obsession is that which helps you achieve better things in life. Many will disagree that obsession is necessary. But when you are obsessed with doing something, the whole process of preparing, your being, your thinking, your dedication, etc., reaches a different level altogether.

Call it Obsession, Positive obsession, Craziness, or Passion. To what degree of commitment can you go to try for your success? Can you plan that level of commitment? For example, when to wake up, how much to work, what skills to gain, what not to eat, and what to eat. How to steal or create time for your own success? Have you thought about this level of obsession? If not, then think and enhance your life.

When you are obsessed, consider implementing a 'Lock-in period'. This means that until you achieve some goals as per planning, say for the next 15 days or so, you will not engage in distractions, such as visiting YouTube or Facebook or any social media site. You will not eat junk food, you will not party, etc. This lock-in period keeps you dedicated.

If obsession is too extreme a word for you then try this question – what constitutes giving 100%? Define your rules and follow them.

Tracking progress – Diary writing

Diary writing is an amazing exercise for improving life. For the present era, I suggest a digital diary connected to the cloud, which will help in capturing important thoughts on the go or while engaged in some activity. Strangely, it is often when you are busy that good ideas emerge.

Write down what you aim to achieve and by when. Prepare a rough plan and track your progress. Perform course corrections. This approach to living is an adventure in itself.

Diary writing is a ritual associated with long-term growth and progress. Time, life, and the external environment will deteriorate our minds and our beings if we don't protect and nourish them.

Therefore, write in your diary, read it, and analyse it. This practice helps give direction to life—read the last three days and plan the next three days every morning and/or evening. You will discover a sense of direction in life. Choose your adventure—determine where you wish to go and work towards it. What's wrong with trying?

Let us also consider Kidlin's Law: If you can write the problem down clearly, then the issue is half solved.

So, cultivate the habit of writing in a diary and referring to it periodically. It aids in memory retention.

Concept of 'Message from the Past'

When you are writing a diary, I recommend that you prepare future-dated pages in your digital diary. In these future-dated pages, write some messages for yourself. Write encouraging messages, ask about the status of some dreams, recommend reading some articles, etc. Here, you can use your imagination regarding what message you want to provide to your future self. Also, the future-dated pages may not be of the very far future. These future-dated pages can be months away or even years away. As you progress through life, you will come across these dated pages when their time comes.

And when you read that message from the past on some future-dated time, you will reassess your direction in life. You will also be encouraged by your past words.

This is also a fun as well as life-transforming activity.

Do you remember when you felt real fulfillment?

Truly feeling the emotions of fulfillment or wholeness is an amazing feeling. Some may try to associate it with some material pleasure, like eating that cake, sleeping on that bed, or truly relaxing on a vacation.

But I would like to propose a different thought and encourage you to ponder over it. We truly feel whole or fulfilled when we are totally devoted to a task; when we are one with the work that we are doing. It is said that busy people are happy people.

Now realise that getting this feeling of fulfillment or feeling whole is so easy to achieve. You just have to do your work with total focus and dedication. And working in this fashion has four advantages too. First of all, you will feel whole and the second advantage is that as you do the work with so much devotion, the quality of your work will be phenomenal. The third advantage is that you will be directly or indirectly rewarded for your work – your work will be noticed.

And the last advantage is that you will gain knowledge and skills when you work with full devotion.

Many have experienced this 'process of feeling whole and fulfilling' but have not truly realised it or made a memory or note of it. With this paragraph, I would like to emphasise how to get that feeling of being whole or fulfilled.

Imaginary Mirror Technique

I came across the imaginary mirror technique at one place and found it very impactful. In this technique, we imagine a large mirror in front of us, and what we see in the mirror is our better version, our ideal version. The surroundings of our image are not an exact reflection of our present environment, but what we want it to look like. We then talk with our reflection and seek guidance from it.

This is a fun technique and should be used sparingly. You can unleash your fantasies; you can try to experience what it could be like if that (success, big achievement, dream come true, etc.) happens. This is a kind of daydreaming; however, at times it can provide some meaningful insights. It has some relation with 'attracting what you desire'.

I have tried this technique many times, and that is why I say that we should use this technique very sparingly. It can make us go crazy at times and provide unrealistic guidance. So, simply use this technique rarely and for fun only.

Being Sensible

Even when you are doing everything right, results may not be in your favour. But don't lose the right path out of disappointment. This is life. It has mysterious ways of revealing things. Keep on studying, keep on moving forward, explore, dream, plan, work on it and remain motivated. When we are sad, we don't realise one thing: life is also abundantly full of opportunities. 'Everything is an opportunity'; develop such an eye and infuse enthusiasm into life. Results are not in our hands; we cannot always have our way. But growth and the will to improve are in our hands.

Understand that success has many forms and life is full of challenges and provides many opportunities. You also need to be an aggressive beast and a ferocious warrior to fight these challenges and to grab the opportunities. This journey, where you face your challenges, work on solutions, and materialise your opportunities, will enrich your personality and being.

You don't choose your circumstances, but you have to deal with them. This is what it is. Everyone has different circumstances. Crying for not having favourable circumstances is foolish; alas, the majority curse the circumstances. The real fun lies in accepting circumstances as they are and trying to improve them relentlessly.

Section 4: The Forever

Chapter 7
GOD AND AFTERLIFE

The book series, 'Conversations with God', written by Neale Donald Walsch, and 'The Laws of the Spirit World' by Khorshed Bhavnagri awakened my interest in God and the afterlife. The existence that we are naturally aware of, i.e., on Earth, may just be a small part of the whole story. My journey regarding belief in God and the afterlife has been a roller coaster ride. I was an atheist initially, then became agnostic, and eventually found myself somewhere as a theist. These shifts were influenced by my level of intellectual maturity and various external factors at different times. I have studied this topic closely and will provide my understanding of it.

What is God?

God is wisdom, direction, and guidance. S/he is a friend and philosopher, an encourager and motivator.

God has no name, no figure. This nameless, bodiless energy comes to those who seek to establish

'Conversations' with him/her. The help is direct or indirect, in God's own time.

As opposed to this, what have people on Earth made of God? They have given him names and allotted him as per religion; people never "converse" with God, rather they simply beg him for things. They don't consider him a friend but rather fear him. They indulge in mindless rituals. And you will be influenced, taught, and pressured to adopt these practices. But don't adopt these practices and seek truth and converse with God. Invite God into your personal space.

Connection with God is a natural gift to everybody. It is always and it is constant. It is through the mental process, silent self-talks, through the ideas that abruptly come to your mind, etc. His blessings are to be understood in 'situations/ circumstances/coincidences/opportunities that help you find true fulfillment, intellect, guidance, wisdom, strength, and wealth'. May you realise this sooner than later.

Everything is Godly, only if you can raise your thinking to that level.

What is beautiful? What is not beautiful?

Where is beauty? Where is no beauty?

Common notions of a beautiful life include comfort, security, abundance, wisdom, etc. And the list goes on. However, there is beauty in the opposite of these too. There is beauty in pain, struggle, difficult situations, challenges, etc. Is it not? Can you find beauty in your difficult times? There is uncertainty, you are exhausted, there is fear, there is no hope and you are in pain. That situation is also beautiful and unique. You operate in that situation too; you make choices in those circumstances too. And once you come out of the misery, you will be thankful and cherish that transforming period forever. Hence, even those struggling times are beautiful. So, tell me, what is not beautiful and where is no beauty?

Similarly, what is Godly? And what is not Godly?

Along similar lines, everything can be Godly too. Many a time we have heard stories of 'Blessings in Disguise', 'Opportunities in Adversity', etc. So, develop yourself to see everything as Godly.

How does God help you? One of the subtle ways of indirect help is through situations. He will expose you to situations – pleasant or unpleasant – which will in turn expose your true nature to yourself. These are beautiful moments, very personal to you only. The realisation will be profound and you will say, I understand what my true nature is after having gone through this situation. In a true sense, one can never say that injustice has been done to him. God asks: what is the problem? If he is really in front of you and asks this, think of the answers. You will realise that pretending to be a victim and that injustice has been done to you is not correct. Everything is justified; it is cause and effect. You can't throw a tantrum at the universe. It gives you exactly what you deeply desire. And this realisation will help you improve (or mend) your being for betterment.

"The Truth, the God, and spirituality" can differ from "religions". Religions and their teachings are mediums to help one understand Truth and God. However, with many misinterpretations and a foolish race for superiority and dominance, there is a rise in cult mentality which pushes extremists to practices that are the exact opposite of the original teachings.

In my opinion, due to the rise of misinterpretations, "The Truth, the God, and spirituality" have become subjects that are to be dealt with in the personal sphere. Have your own conversations with God. And s/he will help you in your pursuit of truth.

"God helps those who help themselves." This is the best advice of all time. First, you have to show willingness to help yourself. You have to take the first step and then only "situations will unfold, opportunities will be aligned on your way, wisdom will be arranged, and direct/indirect help will be provided." This is one of the Truths too.

While discussing this idea with a friend, he asked if it should not be the other way around. That is, for those who cannot help themselves, God should help them. Now that is a very interesting argument. But if you are not helping yourself, that means you are not making efforts or you are not making the choices of progress. In turn, you are expecting God to make the path easier for you. Why would that happen if you yourself don't have any stake in progress?

Another quote about God can be:

"Don't waste your time chasing butterflies. Mend your garden, and the butterflies will come." - Unknown

So, be brave, be honest with yourself, accept the situation as it is, and then take progressive actions.

Some may be sceptical that we are discussing unscientific topics, or that this is the realm of superstition lacking empirical, provable data and evidence. They are slightly correct. However, we also have so many scriptures and recorded personal experiences of many people throughout history, which should catch our attention.

What does being scientific mean? It means to remain open to ideas and not discard these ideas right away just because they don't fit within the boundary of "conclusive analysis" or don't conform to established analytical boundaries. If you are shunning an idea because of your preconceived or preset and pre-educated concept of the scientific mind, then you are not being truly scientific. So, listen to arguments before discarding them. Yes, just don't get influenced by 'too good to be true' or 'magical' claims.

I will touch on this point again in a subsequent paragraph.

Another place where we can meet God

When we give our 100%, when our calendars are packed for certain goals, when we list down dos and don'ts while being on that goal, and when we are positively obsessed with certain things, then magic happens. When we truly give 100%, we meet God.

Another way of saying this is that the address of God lies in positive obsession. If you can be positively obsessed with something, then you will come across God. Try it sometimes and you will love it.

Afterlife

What if I tell you that the afterlife is merely an extension of your current existence – with only slight modifications?

We are often taught some of the following misconceptions about death:

1. Everything comes to an end, and there is just an end.
2. We go to heaven if our deeds or karma were good, and we enjoy a lot.
3. We go to hell if our deeds or karma were bad, and we suffer a lot.

What if I tell you that none of the above is correct?

I do not have evidence, and as a matter of fact, no one has evidence of what life is after death. But being open to the idea that I am going to present, which appears more logical, we can lead a better life. Some may claim that it is equivalent to accepting one lie to make life more meaningful. Maybe. Or maybe it is true as well; we do not know. Let us take our chances.

The idea is that life after death is nothing but an extension of your preset life, with only slight material modification. Your mind will be with you, your mindset, your enthusiasm, and your being will be with you. You will simply enter a different environment. What environment or group of souls you will end up with is determined by how much spiritual progress or self-development progress you have made. And in this environment, you will have to perform certain tasks as per that environment's setup.

Contrary to the popular concept that we may not have to work after we die, this is wrong.

You will have to work in both hell and heaven. More and more difficult work in heaven – such as being selfless, helping others, and improving the overall well-being of the world. And in hell, there will be tasks too – studying, understanding the truth, working on self-development, working hard to take care of your family, strengthening yourself, etc.

Punishment in hell is not in the form of pain but in the form of challenges. And in heaven, the test of enthusiasm and faith is, again, via challenges. So, in all walks of life, accept challenges and move along. Train yourself to deal with any situation, (perceived) injustice, etc.

Yes, I am referencing my learnings from the book 'The Laws of the Spirit World by Khorshed Bhavnagri'. What I have mentioned is not exactly stated in the book, but this is my understanding of the Afterlife. And I find it quite logical too.

Why would there be a sudden change in our being or environment? Why would we be rewarded or punished out of the blue? No, the afterlife is merely an extension of the present life, with slight material modifications. What you sow, you reap. The habits and perceptions you develop while living on Earth, you carry to the afterlife—may it be heaven or hell. And you continue to exist there with these self-qualities.

So here is one conclusion as well, call it our existence or being or awareness, it is actually our prison. We are supposed to be with ourselves for eternity, living through births, hells, and heavens. Without end. There is no true escape from existence. We are just going to run the show forever—either on Earth or in Hell or Heaven. And if we are going to remain with ourselves forever, let us make ourselves more lovable to ourselves and keep on working on the tasks at hand.

How do you know that you are on Earth?

Being scientific means remaining open to all sorts of ideas. We have all agreed to call our living on Earth, but apart from this widely accepted "fact", we really do not know if we are living on Earth, in hell, or in heaven.

What do you think about it?

Work and cosmic slavery

It doesn't matter whether you are on Earth, in hell, or in heaven. You will have a lot of work, a lot of tasks at hand. You will have to put your heart and soul into your work. You will have to work a lot and a bit faster so that you can get some personal time where you will connect with God and converse with him.

You don't have an escape from work; you never had any and you will never have—neither on Earth, nor in hell, nor in heaven. You will have work to do. You will have to work on your situation. You will be put in different situations throughout your existence. And don't think that heaven will have easier tasks, no. There will be more challenging tasks in heaven. Not having an escape from work is nothing but cosmic slavery.

In a nutshell, throughout your existence, whether on Earth, in hell, or in heaven, you will face challenges and a lot of daily work. If you want to do something that you like, then you will have to work faster to find time to do that.

Assume that you will go to hell

Prepare yourself for hell. Don't assume that you will go to heaven. When in hell, prepare yourself for a lot of heartbreaks and disappointments. This is your hell; deal with it. This is what it is. You cannot blame anyone for it. Accept every situation and still maintain a positive mindset. Work on your situations for eternity. Keep moving. This is the knowledge. This is human life. This is the naked truth about us, about our existence, in this life or the afterlife. Don't have a craving to be in heaven. Be ready to adjust and progress anywhere, even in hell. This is the key element, the key attitude, your real asset that you can carry through this life and afterlife.

Impose the afterlife on the present life

Don't think that you are on Earth. Think that you are in the afterlife. Try to be brave, try to do the right thing, and continuously improve and train yourself. The game won't change; you have to change, you have to adapt to all situations, continue with your prayers, and build an attitude that helps you keep going without stopping. This external and internal equation will never change, even in the afterlife. So, build yourself accordingly. Challenges exist even in the afterlife; your attitude (that you develop while living or every moment of life) is your true asset throughout your existence, and you cannot be tired of it either.

Section 5: Just Be

Chapter 8
PREPARE YOUR OWN ISLAND – REMAIN SECRET

You have seen how the world has become in the initial chapters. However hard one may try to convince you otherwise, your dreams, ambitions, and plans; your wealth, success, and happiness are not taken positively in this world. It is a bitter trait of the present world.

But, let us use this observation for our benefit. Never let anyone know what you are up to or what your overall state is. Just keep it a secret.

This approach of secrecy has dual benefits:

1st is that you won't develop an ego but, on the contrary, you will develop a distinctive, mysterious, and charismatic personality and aura.

2nd, you will be away from the evil eye or unnecessary obstacles which might be created by others.

This is not a new idea; many happy, intelligent, and wealthy people are using it. No one needs to know anything about you. You also don't need to know what is happening outside. Live a secretive life. Get educated, become intelligent, become successful and wealthy; then reduce information inflow. In reality, you don't need to know who your political leaders are, what they are planning, what the current developments are, etc. Turn off the news, delete social media accounts, unsubscribe from newspapers, etc. Visit the world only when you need to. Choose a career or work in which you don't need to keep track of all the unnecessary information. You have to pretend to blend in whatever crowd you are in, whatever economic or political atmosphere you are in, pretend that you exist and are part of the crowd but secretly build an empire for yourself and your family.

The world is not a very good place. It has a problem with your happiness. So, don't show it. Show instead what it wants to see, and pretend that you are an average and mediocre person. And don't talk about your ambitions or dreams, ever. There is no need, actually. Even after becoming successful, there is no need to declare that. Just do your stuff and progress in silence with your family.

Your island

Living in such a way is akin to living on an island. You will physically be in the crowd but will remain indifferent to them. Your life will not be affected by anything around you. You will appear as an average person and part of the crowd. That is why even the crowd will be indifferent to you. Maintain this façade while you build something great inside. You will be happy and successful.

Having your own island will give you privacy and your own time. Getting both of these has become a luxury nowadays. In our own time, we need some deep silence. Deep silence and meditation will nourish your soul. This silence is necessary and freely available. There is no escape; you will crave total silence inside the mind at various points in life.

Hence, create your own island and flourish on it.

The joy of secret mission

Now that we have understood the importance of remaining secretive, if we start keeping our various endeavours confidential, it can become a joyful activity. Imagine this: People around you do not know what you are up to. And you are, in your own time, working on some project secretly. You complete the project and then start receiving recognition and rewards. Even then, you don't disclose it, but people will come to know about it eventually. When such a sudden shift or achievement is realised, people will truly understand your true worth.

But if you disclose what you are working on while you have not finished but are still in process, then:

- First, people will not acknowledge it.
- Second, people will discourage you.
- Third, people will not value you and your project.

Hence, don't tell anyone about anything. There is really no need. Just share it with someone when you need some genuine help or guidance. Otherwise, enjoy your secret missions.

The Angel's Condition: "You will have everything you dreamed of, but you cannot tell anyone about it on your own."

Somehow, I have come to understand that the spiritual forces which provide wealth and fulfillment include a clause stating, "You will have everything you dreamed of, but you cannot tell anyone about it on your own." This is because when you keep some things secret, the energy of your dream and your project is not corrupted; it remains pure and it grows, it gets nourished, and finally, it comes into being. So, understand this condition of the Angel.

Section 6: Last Words

Chapter 9
SUMMARY THROUGH IDEAS

This is the last chapter of this book. Here, we will summarise the ideas discussed throughout. You will read about ideas that have already been mentioned in the book and others not directly mentioned so far, but which align with the overall theme of the book. This chapter can also act as a quick reference when you want to refresh your memory at different points in life, or when you feel lost, or when you feel like revising the knowledge that you gained from this book.

1. "Doing your best is the only option, even if it results in failure." — 'Eddie The Eagle' (Movie)
2. "The day you think there are no improvements to be made is a sad one for any player." — Lionel Messi
3. "My ambition is to always become better and better." — Lionel Messi (What a great ambition!)
4. "Discipline sets you free."

5. "Mind is everything, what you think you become." — Lord Buddha
6. "Mann Kara Re Prasanna, Sarva Siddhiche Kaaran" — Sant Tukaram. This means, make your mind fresh (purified), this is the cause of all prosperity and achievements.
7. "The greatest version of you is not the 'I can do anything' version of you. The greatest version of you is 'the disciplined version of you.'" — Ben Lionel Scott Videos
8. "Just do it." — Nike
9. "Push yourself to the verge of craziness, passion, and obsession. That mental state is earned, it's unique and in a way, blissful — no one will teach that."
10. "There is no finish line. You are never supposed to stop. You are never supposed to reduce the intensity." — Ben Lionel Scott Videos
11. "The greatest discovery of my generation is that a human being can alter his life by altering his attitude." — William James
12. "There is no point in living if not with the right mentality."
13. "It is the mindset (or mentality) that has value, not the results."
14. "An entire sea of water can't sink a ship unless it gets inside the ship. Similarly, the negativity

of the world can't put you down unless you allow it to get inside you."

15. "The only impossible journey is the one you never begin." — Tony Robbins

16. "What appears pressure and difficult for others (discipline, work ethics, being ambitious, etc.) is the way of life for some."

17. युद्ध ही तो वीर का प्रमाण है, जो लड़ सका है वही तो महान है – Yudha hi to vir ka praman hai – Jo Lad Saka Hai Wohi Toh Mahaan Hai — Lyrics from Piyush Mishra's song, Arambh Hai Prachand. Translation: Battle is the validation of a warrior and the one who can fight is actually great. [Greatness lies in giving the fight]. — Lyrics from Piyush Mishra's song, 'Arambh Hai Prachand'.

18. "Obstacles are not in the way; they are the way."

19. "New life starts with a new mind."

20. "Your whole idea about yourself is borrowed—from those who have no idea of who they are themselves." – Osho

21. "Greatness is not in the end or results, but in every day."

22. "The essence of 'Effort' itself is beautiful and that is why the one who puts in effort becomes beautiful." – Unknown

23. "We all are on a spiritual journey, period. We all are going to end in the same place, if there is such a thing." – Jim Carrey

24. "Fear disguised as practicality" – That is why what we really want seems impossibly out of reach and ridiculous to expect. So, we never dare to ask the universe for it. Jim Carrey says he is the proof that you can ask the universe for it.

25. "Only now and this moment is real. Where really are the other moments? Even the thoughts I am having of the past are my memories of present moments."

26. "If you are not finding joy and enthusiasm in difficult and adverse situations, then you are losing, spirituality in particular and life in general."

27. "Have a desire for glory."

28. "God asks: What is the problem?"

29. "It is not people who are great or successful, but their minds."

30. "I can find myself only in the present moment."

31. "The clock is always ticking. Not being closer to your goal even after days or hours is a nightmare." – Ben Lionel Scott Videos

32. "Life is the grind. Work every waking hour for your goal or greatness." – Ben Lionel Scott Videos

33. "It is not what happens outside that determines success, it is what happens within you that determines success." – Ben Lionel Scott Videos

34. "Don't call the world dirty because you forgot to clean your glasses." – Aaron Hill

35. "To be born is not your choice; to die is not your choice, but to live the way you want is definitely your choice."

36. "Being born in poverty is not your fault, but dying poor is your fault."

37. "Being born rich is your fate, but not dying rich is your stupidity."

38. "Whatever there is in life, accept it, know it, and live it. From this acceptance will come the transformation." – Osho

39. "Aaj bhi jo sacchai ki raah par chalte hain, unka rath Shri Krishna chalate hain." Translation: Those who still walk the path of truth, their chariot is led by Lord Shri Krishna.

40. "The only meaningful and satisfying conversations you will have are the ones that happen with God."

41. "You meet your real self after closing your eyes."

42. "The present moment is real and it is a replica of your life."

43. "Treat others the way you want to be treated."

44. "Repeat anything enough times, it will appear as truth."

45. "God helps those who help themselves. If you don't help yourself, God won't."

46. "It is not what is outside, what matters is what is inside."

47. "The moment you stop tapascharya (hard work), your success will end." – Ravana

48. "The difference between good leaders and great leaders is not an issue of 'more'. They're fundamentally different people."

49. "We spend too much time trying to be 'good' when good is often merely average. To be great, we must be different. And that doesn't come from trying to follow society's vision of what is best, because society doesn't always know what it needs. More often, being the best means just being the best version of you. As John Stuart Mill remarked, "That so few now dare to be eccentric, marks the chief danger of our time." In the right environment,

bad can be good and odd can be beautiful. – Ben Lionel Scott Videos.

50. "Optimists tell themselves a story that may not be true, but it keeps them going, often allowing them to beat the odds." – Psychologist Shelley Taylor says that "a healthy mind tells itself flattering lies." The pessimists were more accurate and realistic, and they ended up depressed.

51. "Don't waste your time chasing butterflies. Mend your garden, and the butterflies will come." – Unknown

52. "Dig deep, and make your own decisions. The wisdom of crowds is not just imperfect, but sometimes, highly misleading."

53. "Nobody is going to believe in your story until you win, so win." – Unknown

54. "Don't be afraid of ten thousand miles ahead. Just by walking step by step, you can cover ten thousand miles easily." – Osho

55. "Circumstances in the afterlife are not going to be any different than present life. Things remain almost the same. So, build yourself every moment. There is no magic after death. Existence is an ever-going journey. You can't avoid what fate has brought you. Accepting, solving, and moving forward are our only options, in life and afterwards."

56. "You can't throw a tantrum to the universe. It gives you exactly what you deeply desire."

57. "You will see what you are looking for."

58. "The mind is heaven, the mind is hell, and the mind has the capacity to become either." – Osho

59. "If you crave something, that is what you are not going to get soon enough, it will be delayed. What you crave for and especially show the desperation for, will be made difficult by cosmic forces. Intense desires are seemingly met with obstacles or delays."

60. "Murphy's Law: The more you fear something, the more it will happen."

61. "Discipline, remembering planning, and training are musts for every day. Otherwise, in this world of distractions, there is no limit to drifting away."

62. "Finish all the work—small or big—on your list as soon as possible. This is the process of earning time for yourself, and you will have to do that work anyhow."

63. "It is easy to complete 95% of the work but it's difficult to complete 100% of the work."

64. "When you are giving up, someone is still going."

65. "The most important decision we make is whether we believe we live in a friendly or hostile universe." – Albert Einstein
66. "If you keep doing what you've been doing, you'll keep getting what you've been getting."
67. "Gilbert's Law: The biggest problem at work is that no one tells you what to do."
68. "Falkland's Law: When you don't have to make a decision, then don't make a decision."
69. "Walson's Law: If you put knowledge and intelligence first at all times, the money keeps coming in."
70. "Kidlin's Law: If you write the problem down clearly, then the matter is half solved."
71. "Build your dreams brick by brick."
72. "The address of God lies on the street of positive obsession."
73. "The biggest lie in the world is, 'I don't have time for this', whereas the reality is, 'You don't have Will for it'."
74. "Life gets easier if you get stronger; otherwise, life will keep on getting harder and harder."
75. "The whole world is nothing but a mirror." – Osho

ABOUT ME

I am Nikhil Pramod Bhandare, currently serving as an Officer in the State Bank of India, having joined this prestigious institution in March 2021 as an SBI PO—a role widely regarded as one of the most difficult exams to crack in India.

Originally from Yavatmal district in the Vidarbha region of Maharashtra, my educational journey included schooling up to 10th grade in Yavatmal, completion of my 12th in Hyderabad, and graduation from BITS Pilani, Rajasthan. From a young age, I've been a curious soul with an inclination to spirituality and finding meaning in life. I continued my observations on the meaning of life, relation of thoughts on our surroundings, decoding propagandas, pursuit of truth, etc., as I progressed through the regular channel of schooling—graduation—preparation for competitive examinations—job hunt—and finally in service.

Getting a good job in the present time is really a big struggle. And this struggle further makes you a philosopher. After my graduation, I prepared for various competitive examinations in India, such as UPSC civil services, UPSC Central Armed Police Force, MPSC and Bank and Regulatory Body exams. I used to get mixed successes in these examinations, such as writing four mains and facing one UPSC civil services interview, two UPSC CAPF interviews and numerous other mains stage (that is second stage of selection) of many exams, but I never got the final rank or posting till the year 2021. This was a struggle for almost a decade.

During these years of preparation, I also engaged in tutoring and content development on a contractual basis at coaching institutes like Unique Academy. Alongside friends such as Mr. Rizwan Shaik (IAS), Mr. Rickey Agrawal (IIS and now IPS), and Mr. Kunal Nage (Officer in EPFO), I co-authored the book 'UPSC Mains Paper Solutions 2018 (Gs Papers 1,2,3 & 4)' for Unique Academy and contributed to 'The Civil Service Guidance Program' at Akola Collectorate Office.

Even during my hustle, my observations and study of mind, thoughts, materialization and overall pursuit of truth never stopped.

The phase of 'No success or struggle' (let's not call it the 'phase of failure') is hard for the aspirant and more so for the family members. Lack of identity and income, passing years, rising age, uncertainty about success and societal pressure will demoralize anyone. In such circumstances, self-motivation, self-encouragement, a positive mindset and enthusiasm are the only solutions And I practised these during my struggle time.

I developed a habit of writing my personal diary in the digital format which is based on cloud technology. I used to note down my observations and experiences in my diary and then analyse them. As the diary was digital and the data was on the cloud, I could note the thoughts or conclusions as and when they came to my mind and make changes either through mobile or laptop without losing my data. This book is the result of all that hard work.

However, what really triggered me to finalize the book was the birth of my daughter. I knew that I had a fairly good analysis of life, I wanted to pass it to her. I also know that what I want to teach her won't be taught in school or anywhere else. And that inspired me to write this book. I am finally content that she will know what her Papa has left behind for her.

I also hope that this book will help other readers too.

For feedback, suggestions, or questions, I can be reached at riselifehelp@gmail.com. Let's thrive together in this life and beyond.

www.ingramcontent.com/pod-product-compliance
Lightning Source LLC
La Vergne TN
LVHW091054150826
845673LV00002B/576

* 9 7 9 8 8 9 4 1 5 3 8 2 7 *